I0394256

Contents

INTRODUCTION.. 3
HOW SHOULD THE HANDBOOK AND THE WORKSHEETS BE USED?............................ 4
BEFORE BEGINNING THE URBAN FARM BUSINESS PLAN 5
USING THE URBAN FARM BUSINESS PLAN HANDBOOK 6
OVERVIEW 7
INTRODUCTION.. 7
VISION STATEMENT 7
MISSION STATEMENT 8
GOALS 8
ORGANIZATION AND MANAGEMENT 9
MARKETING STRATEGY 10
INTRODUCTION... 10
MARKET 10
        Customers 11
PRODUCT 12
DISTRIBUTION 12
SALES 13
        Pricing 13
        Sales Volume 13
COMPETITION 14
PROMOTION 14
OPERATING STRATEGY 15
INTRODUCTION... 15
CROP MANAGEMENT 15
YIELD 16
PHYSICAL RESOURCE NEEDS 16
HUMAN RESOURCE NEEDS 17
REGULATION AND POLICY 17
FINANCIAL STRATEGY 19
INTRODUCTION... 19
EXPENSES 19
INCOME 19
PROFIT AND LOSS 20
FIXED ASSETS 20
FUNDING REQUIREMENTS 20
RISK MANAGEMENT 21
EXECUTIVE SUMMARY 22
APPENDIX A: LIST OF PROVIDED WORKSHEETS A-1
APPENDIX B: EXAMPLE WORKSHEETS B-1

Introduction

As communities look for sustainable reuses for brownfield and other abandoned properties and opportunities to provide healthier food choices to the community, interest in establishing community gardens and other forms of farming has been growing in urban areas. Urban farms, however, present unique challenges that are different from conventional agricultural development.

Developed land often has a history of uses that may have affected the quality of the soil (e.g., environmental contamination, building debris and other fill material unfit for plant growth) that may require substantial site preparation (e.g., environmental cleanup, demolition, or placement of topsoil) or special growing techniques (e.g., raised growing beds, vertical gardens). Urban farms typically need to address security issues for the crops, buildings and tools. In many cases, urban farm development and operating practices will have to account for the proximity of residential and/or commercial neighbors and the compatibility of the farm operations with these neighbors. In addition, the success of an urban farm may depend on a diversity of products as opposed to a single crop and volunteer labor to support the start-up and initial operations.

As urban farming moves towards income-earning or food-producing activities, it is important to develop a plan for the start-up and operation of the business regardless of whether it is intended to be a for-profit business or a non-profit business. A business plan provides a road map that not only serves as an internal planning tool, but can be used to provide information to external stakeholders important to the successful start up and operation of the business such as investors and funding sources. It is used to map out the strategies for the start up and operation of a business and to track progress of that business against its goals.

> ### What is an Urban Farm?
>
> An urban farm is a part of a local food system where food is cultivated and produced within an urban area and marketed to consumers within that urban area. Urban farming can also include animal husbandry (e.g., breeding and raising livestock), beekeeping, aquaculture (e.g., fish farming), aquaponics (e.g., integrating fish farming and agriculture), and non-food products such as producing seeds, cultivating seedlings, and growing flowers. It can be characterized in terms of the geographic proximity of a producer to the consumer, sustainable production and distribution practices.
>
> Urban farms can take a variety of forms including non-profit gardens and for-profit businesses. They can provide jobs, job training, and health education, and they can contribute to better nutrition and health for the community by providing locally grown, fresh produce and other products. In addition, urban farms can also contribute to the revitalization of abandoned or underutilized urban land, social and economic benefits to urban communities, and beneficial impacts on the urban landscape.

Through EPA's Office of Brownfields and Land Revitalization and the Partnership for Sustainable Communities, technical assistance was provided to support the development of a business plan for an urban farm in Toledo. The technical assistance was intended to support the Toledo Community Development Corporation (CDC) in achieving its vision to reuse a two-plus-acre former industrial site as an economically viable and accessible source of fresh locally grown fruits and vegetables, jobs and job training, and education on growing and preserving fresh produce and improved health through better diet for the community.

The project resulted in the development of two products that will be used in Toledo, but also have wider application to brownfield and other communities working on land revitalization across the country that are seeking alternative sustainable reuses that can improve access to fresh and healthy food, and related food shed economics and market conditions in local areas:
- Urban Farm Business Plan Handbook.
- Urban Farm Business Plan Worksheets.

HOW SHOULD THE HANDBOOK AND THE WORKSHEETS BE USED?

The **Urban Farm Business Plan Handbook** (this document) provides guidance for developing a business plan for the startup and operation of an urban farm.[1] It focuses on food and non-food related cultivated agriculture. The information provided is applicable regardless of whether the farm is to be operated as a non-profit or for-profit business.

More specifically, it describes what information should be collected, evaluated, and presented in each section of the business plan. The Handbook is designed to be used side-by-side with the accompanying Urban Farm Business Plan Worksheets. As the Handbook describes each section of the business plan, there are references to worksheets that should be filled out in order to fully develop that section of the business plan. A list of all of the provided worksheets is in Appendix A. The handbook also includes example worksheets to help users understand how to fill in the worksheets, in Appendix B. While the example worksheets do not represent a complete set of worksheets and include hypothetical information, they do provide a useful example of the level of detail and background research required to develop a business plan. Blank worksheets can be found in the Urban Farm Business Plan Worksheet files, described below.

The **Urban Farm Business Plan Worksheets** provides a framework in which to compile and organize the information needed to draft a business plan. There are two files that comprise the Worksheets:

1. Urban Farm Business Plan Worksheet.doc (Microsoft (MS) Word®). This file contains blank worksheets that when completed will provide the information needed to write a business plan. Worksheets 1-16, 18-22, and 28-29 are contained in this file. A list of all worksheets and in which file they are located is provided in Appendix A.

2. Urban Farm Business Plan Worksheet.xls (Microsoft (MS) Excel®). This file contains spreadsheets with formulas to help calculate expenditures and revenue. Worksheets 17 and 23-27 are contained in this file. A list of all worksheets and in which file they are located is provided in Appendix A.

The information presented in the following sections of this handbook is intended to be representative of the information needed for the development of a business plan; however, the specific goals and plans for any individual farm may require more or less information be provided for their particular plan.

The Urban Farm Business Plan Handbook and Worksheets are available on EPA's urban agriculture website: www.epa.gov/brownfields/urbanag/.

---

[1] This handbook has been prepared for informational purposes only. Vita Nuova has relied upon outside sources for information and data presented in this report. Although all best efforts were used to confirm the information and data presented in this report and to complete this report, no representation or warranties are made as to the timeliness, accuracy or completeness of the information contained herein or that the actual results will conform to any projections or recommendations contained herein. All areas are approximate. Any reliance upon this material shall be without any liability or obligation on the part of Vita Nuova LLC, SRA International, or the U.S. EPA.

Before Beginning the Urban Farm Business Plan

Before beginning the development of your business plan, think about the primary reasons for starting an urban farm. Documenting your reasons for starting the farm will help you focus the business plan and identify the issues, the resources and the expertise that will be needed to develop the business plan. Finally, think about the values that you bring to the business and the values that are important to the success of the business.

Consider the following questions:

- Do you have crop growing or farm experience that will assist in your farm operations or will you need to secure that expertise elsewhere?
- Will you be involved with food production, animal husbandry, aquaculture, aquaponics, or non-food products or some combination of products?
- Do you have a property for your urban farm or are you in the process of selecting a location?
- Are you developing the farm as a community-based, non-profit business that will involve community members in the operation?
- Are you developing the farm as a for-profit business and income source?
- Are you developing the farm as a family-run business and source of income?
- Is there a particular expertise or product that you want to commercialize?
- Are you creating the farm to provide produce for another business, such as an institution or restaurant?
- Who will be part of your planning team?
- Do you have the expertise to develop marketing, operating, human resource, and financial strategies necessary for the business plan or to help in the start up of the business?
- Are you going to need expertise to address environmental and cleanup issues that may be associated with an urban property you intend to farm?
- Do you need to hire expertise to develop the strategies, conduct surveys, or plan the development?
- Do you need financial resources to obtain this expertise?
- Is there an economic motivation for this farm?
- Are you hoping to generate a profit, break-even, or will the farm require a source of charitable income?
- Is the farm to be community-focused?
- To what extent are environmental issues related to the operation of the farm a consideration, such as organic fertilizers and resource use?

Use *Worksheet # 1 (Before You Begin)* to document your reasons, expertise and resource needs.[2]

---

[2] Please refer to Appendix A: Worksheet Summary List to identify the file in which each worksheet is contained.

Using the Urban Farm Business Plan Handbook

The business plan is divided into six sections:

- Executive Summary.
- Overview.
- Organization and Management.
- Marketing Strategy.
- Operating Strategy.
- Financial Strategy.

The following sections in this handbook address each of these sections of the business plan. In addition, blank worksheets are provided in the Urban Farm Business Plan Worksheets (available on EPA's urban agriculture website (www.epa.gov/brownfields/urbanag) to help identify the information typically required under the topics discussed in that section and to document the information needed to develop the business plan. Example worksheets with information filled in are provided in Appendix B.

The sections in the handbook are provided in the order in which they should appear in the final business plan, with the exception of the Executive Summary section which is developed last but should appear first in the final business plan. The development of the business plan will not necessarily follow this order, depending on the information readily available for each urban farm project. It is important to note that the development of a business plan may require access to the appropriate expertise to adequately develop the information necessary to address the topics contained in the business plan.

To begin developing a business plan, define your vision, mission, and goals of the business as discussed in the Overview section of this handbook. The vision, mission, and goal statements provide the conceptual outline for the urban farm business. These statements should be considered draft or preliminary and subject to change as the completion of the remaining sections of the business plan may suggest changes to these statements are appropriate. Next define the organization and management structure for the farm as discussed in the Organization and Management section of this handbook.

Based on the vision, mission, and goals, discuss your understanding of the market and potential products of the farm. In many cases, a marketing study may need to be conducted to identify the potential markets and products most appropriate for the farm. Using the information about the market, the marketing strategy is defined as discussed in the Marketing Strategy section of this handbook.

Building on the marketing strategy, the next step is to define the operations and human resources necessary to achieve the marketing strategy. The information about the operation of the farm is used to develop the operating strategy as discussed in the section of this handbook.

Finally, the executive summary section is developed to summarize the key concepts of the business plan as discussed in the Financial Strategy section of this handbook.

Overview

The overview introduces the reader to the business plan, provides your vision and mission for the farm, and summarizes your goals for the farm. The overview is divided into four sections:

- Introduction.
- Vision Statement.
- Mission Statement.
- Goals.

Santa Fe Farmer's Market, Santa Fe, New Mexico

INTRODUCTION

The introduction describes the purpose of the business plan and the key issues addressed by the plan. It provides the reader with an understanding of what information is contained in the business plan and a general description of the plan development process.

Consider the following questions:

- Is the business plan an internal organizing tool, a tool for communicating outside the proposed business, or a combination of both?
- Is there information that is missing or unable to be identified at this stage of the planning process?
- Who are the members of your business planning team?
- Who was involved in the planning process?
- What is the planned size of the company and is future growth anticipated?
- What is the time frame considered in the business plan? (At minimum, the plan should consider a 5-year time frame.)
- Is it to be a for-profit or non-profit business?
- Are there potential risks for the start up of this business?

Use *Worksheet # 2 (Introduction)* to document the information to include in the introduction.

VISION STATEMENT

The vision statement is an inspirational statement that describes your vision for the future of the farm and how your values will be incorporated into the farm. It focuses on the future and provides a direction for the farm and the community in which it operates. It provides clear decision-making criteria.

Consider the following questions:

- What economic, environmental, or community values are important to the success of the farm?
- In a general sense, what products or services do you expect to provide?
- How will the community benefit from these products or services?
- How will operating practices enhance the environment?

Use *Worksheet # 3 (Vision)* to document the information to include in the vision statement.

MISSION STATEMENT

The mission statement is a simple statement that communicates the fundamental purpose and expectations for the farm to its customers and others outside of the business. It is a set of guiding principles that describes the overall goals of the business and serves as a benchmark. It incorporates meaningful and measurable criteria addressing concepts such as values of the business, public image, the target market, products or services, the geographic extent of the business, and expectations of growth and profitability. It provides an understanding of what the business aspires to be and what the business will be known for in the future.

Use *Worksheet # 4 (Mission)* to document the information to include in the mission statement.

GOALS

The goals describe what is to be achieved by the business in the future. Goals can be expressed in terms of time, such as short-term and long-term goals. For a start-up business, short-term goals may be focused on the startup of the business and achieving a certain level of production income. Long-term goals can reflect plans for growth. Goals address potential products, what the farm will look like, who will be involved in operations, and your expectations from the business. The goals reflect what you would like to achieve and when you would like to achieve them. They do not identify how this will be accomplished. Clearly identified goals can motivate, help to mitigate conflict, and direct limited resources.

Use *Worksheet # 5 (Goals)* to document the information to include in the goal discussion.

Organization and Management

Describe the ownership structure of the business and how the business will be organized and managed. If you decide to create a corporation, a non-profit, a limited liability company, or a partnership, you will need to register your business with the state. Check with your state's requirements for organizing a business and registering your business name. In addition, you will need to register your business with the IRS and state and local revenue agencies and receive a tax identification number or permit.

Consider the following questions:

- What will be the legal structure of your organization (e.g., sole proprietorship, partnership, limited liability company, corporation, non-profit, cooperative)?
- How will the business management be organized?
- Will there be a single farm manager to oversee all business operations or multiple managers to oversee various business segments (e.g., marketing, operations, finance, human resources)? Where a multiple manager structure is anticipated, a simple organization chart may be useful to explain the organization.
- Who will be the principal or key managers who will run the business?
- What unique skills do they bring to the business and what will be their duties and responsibilities?
- Will there be an overseeing board or board of directors?
- What will be the composition of such a board and what, if any, role will members of the board take in the business?
- How will the principals, key managers, or board members be compensated?
- Are there any administrative expenses associated with the management or oversight of this business?

Use *Worksheet # 6 (Organization and Management)* to document information about the organization and management of your business.

Marketing Strategy

Barn, Lynchburg Grows! Lynchburg, Virginia

Defining a strategy for marketing and sales is the most important part of your business plan. If a market does not exist or if a workable approach for getting your product to the market has not been identified, you will not meet your goals or expectations. The development of your marketing strategy will require an understanding of the market, including the demand for your product, the potential customers, and the potential competitors. In developing a marketing strategy, you need to convince yourself, as well as the reader of the business plan, that there is a viable market for your product. The marketing strategy is divided into seven sections:

- Introduction.
- Market.
- Product.
- Distribution.
- Competition.
- Promotion.

INTRODUCTION

The introduction to the marketing section summarizes for the reader:

- The potential customers for the farm (Market).
- The products that will be produced and sold (Products).
- Where and how the products will be made available to the customers (Distribution).
- The competitors (Competition).
- How the customers will be made aware of the farm and its products (Promotion).

It should also describe the approach that was taken in developing the marketing strategy.

MARKET

The market section provides an analysis of the market to identify your potential customers or target market. To identify your potential customers, you will first need to have a general understanding of the environment in which your business will operate. Describe the economic factors, such as inflation, unemployment, interest rates, and income that affect a potential customer's purchasing power and spending patterns. Income, for example, will affect a consumer's ability to purchase and the price you will be able to charge for your product. Discuss the demographic factors that describe your potential customers. Demographics provide information on the size, location, age, income, and other statistics about potential consumers. Discuss the social and cultural factors that will influence or impact your business. Social and cultural factors refer to the basic values, perceptions, preferences, and behaviors of your potential customers. They could include preferences on the types of crops to be grown, the ease of purchase of the product, perceptions of organic versus chemical-based production, and impact on the immediate neighborhood. Finally, discuss any voids in the market that your farm will fill.

Consider the following questions:

- What are the significant regulatory requirements that need to be addressed or that will impact your business?
- Who are your potential customers (e.g., households, commercial businesses)?
- Where are your customers located (i.e., within easy transportation or long distances)?
- How likely are they to buy your product (is the project unique or of superior quality)?
- Is there a particular crop that you will grow that is not easily accessible to the consumer?
- Is fresh, organically grown produce easily accessible to the consumer?

Use *Worksheet # 7 (Market Analysis)* to document information to include in the market section.

Customers

Considering the market analysis, describe the customers that your farm will target and how your offerings will meet their needs. Where appropriate, divide the larger target market into submarkets (market segments), such as direct marketing to individual households or business-to-business marketing. Identify the market segments to be targeted. Describe the size and geographic location of each market segment. For example, distance from the business, number of households, commercial establishments or institutional establishments, and likely purchase volume. Discuss the specific characteristics or demographics that define the target customers in each segment, such as age, gender, and income. Discuss the attributes of the market segment related to personality, values, attitudes, interests, or lifestyles. Describe the specific needs and preferences of the market segment that the farm will target.

Consider the following questions:

- Are there trends and/or market conditions that were considered for each market segment?
- Is there a specific product that will appeal to the market segment?
- What motivates buying decisions in each market segment?
- What evidence is there that potential customers in each market segment want the product?

Use *Worksheet # 8 (Market Segments)* to document information about the customers and market segments. Complete a worksheet for each market segment.

PRODUCT

Using information developed in the market analysis about the customer values, needs, and preferences, describe the products to be offered and how they will compete in the target market. This could be a list of specific products (collard greens) or a list of general classes of products (greens). Product offerings should also include the seasonal availability of the products. Describe the specific characteristics of the product that meet the needs of the target market. For example, the market segment desires fresh, organically grown produce from local suppliers or the specific product is not available in the current market. Discuss why the products offered to each market segment are unique. Attributes such as locally grown, organically produced, and price serve to differentiate a product and make it unique. Finally, describe why the business is different from its competitors. Attributes such as being a local employer, accessibility to customers, and partnerships with local businesses help to describe the uniqueness of your business.

Consider the following questions:

- What products will be offered?
- What is the product availability (seasonal offerings)?
- Why would a customer prefer your product to a competitor's?
- What differentiates your product in the target market?
- How does your product differ from that of your competitor's?
- What are the strengths and weaknesses of the product?

Use *Worksheet # 9 (Product)* to document information about your product. Complete a worksheet for each market segment.

DISTRIBUTION

Getting your product to the market will be a critical component of your marketing strategy. Perishable products will need to be delivered or sold to customers within a short period of time after harvest or stored. The quality of crops and customer perception will depend on the quality and freshness of your product. Describe how your product will get to each market segment. Discuss the handling of the product from harvest to sale to the customers in each market segment including any options for storage of the product prior to sale.

Consider the following questions:

- Are products to be packaged for distribution (salad mixes), secondary products (salsa or preserves), or distributed in bulk crates or bushels?
- Are products going to be stored for later distribution?
- Will product be distributed direct from the harvest to the customer?
- How will your product be sold?
- Will the distribution be through direct marketing, such as community supported agriculture, farmers' markets, home delivery services, Internet sales, pick-your-own, or will the products be marketed through an intermediary distributor (e.g., retailers, wholesalers, brokers, or cooperatives)?
- How will product quality be maintained during storage and distribution?
- Why was a particular method of distribution selected for a market segment?
- Are there seasonal issues that will affect the supply of product to a market segment or the distribution of the product to a market segment?
- What will you do with product that is not sold or delivered?

Use *Worksheet # 10 (Distribution)* to document information about your approach to storage and distribution. Complete a worksheet for each market segment.

SALES

Using information developed in the market analysis about the average product consumption, geographic location, and customer attributes, needs, and preferences, develop simple sales projections for each market segment. Since various crops may be seasonal, describe when and how long product will be available for each market segment. For example, products may be available for a market segment all year or only on a seasonal basis.

Pricing

To develop your sales projections, consider the prevailing prices for the products to be sold and your strategy for pricing these products. Describe the pricing strategy for each market segment and how your strategy compares with the competition. Finally, discuss why the selected pricing strategy will be effective in the market segment.

Consider the following questions:

- What are the prevailing market prices for similar products?
- What is the sensitivity of demand to price?
- Will customers be willing to pay higher prices for your offering?
- How will the product be priced for each market segment? Will pricing be based on what your competitors are charging, on the cost of producing the crop plus a percentage for profit, on a price determined by a market study, or some other form of pricing strategy?
- Is there evidence that the target market segment will accept the price?

Use *Worksheet # 11 (Pricing)* to document information about your approach to pricing. Complete a worksheet for each market segment.

Sales Volume

Estimate the potential volume of sales for each market segment. This discussion will require an estimate for each market segment of the number of potential customers in your planned market area and the number (or percentage) of these potential customers that will be needed to sustain the anticipated volume of product. The potential sales volume will be the product of the potential number of customers times the potential volume for each customer. Describe any assumptions that were made about the market segment and volume estimates. Identify any research that was conducted or used to develop information about each market segment.

Use *Worksheet # 12 (Sales Volume)* to document information about potential sales volumes. Complete a worksheet for each market segment.

COMPETITION

Describe the competition for each market segment and how the business will be positioned to compete in each market segment. Summarize the products they provide, the characteristics of their products, and pricing for their products. Discuss the advantages your business will have over your competitors in each market segment. Discuss the disadvantages your business will have to the competitors in each market segment. Discuss how your business will distinguish itself from competitors. Finally, discuss whether competitors are expected to respond to your entry into the market and how quickly and effectively the competitors may be able to respond.

Consider the following questions:

- Who are the competitors for each product segment?
- Is your product of a higher quality, better meets the needs of the consumer, or is more accessible?
- Are your competitors established in the market?
- Do they offer a greater variety of products?
- Will your pricing be competitive with your competitors?
- Will product distribution be an issue?
- Why will customers switch to or select this business over a competitor?
- Will your business provide higher quality product, greater variety, better service, lower prices?

Use *Worksheet # 13 (Competition)* to document information about competitors. Complete a worksheet for each market segment.

PROMOTION

Discuss how you will gain access to the market segments and distribution channels. Describe how you will communicate your message about the product or business. Discuss what you want to communicate to your customers. Discuss how much you expect to spend on advertising and communication.

Consider the following questions:

- How will potential customers find out about your product?
- What approaches will be used to promote your farm and its products?
- Will you advertise the product, the business or company image, or both?
- Will you contact potential customers directly or use display ads in magazines or newspapers, mailings, flyers, catalogues, Internet, social media, programs promoting locally grown products, or some combination?
- Do you want to communicate your business values, the product you are supplying, product quality, production practices (organic, local), price, availability, or some combination?
- How often will customers be contacted through advertising and communications?
- Why do you believe that the selected approach will be effective in reaching the target customer?

Use *Worksheet # 14 (Promotion)* to document information about your approach to promotion. Complete a worksheet for each market segment.

Operating Strategy

The operating strategy is divided into five sections:

- Introduction.
- Crop Management.
- Size and Capacity.
- Physical Resource Needs.
- Human Resource Needs.
- Regulation and Policy.

Brownfields to Farmers Market Shelton, Connecticut

INTRODUCTION

The introduction for the Operating Strategy section summarizes for the reader:

- The approach for cultivating and harvesting the crops (Crop Management).
- The estimated production capacity of the farm (Size and Capacity).
- The physical resources needed to operate the farm (Physical Resources).
- The human resources needed to operate the farm (Human Resources).
- The regulatory issues and requirements that need to be addressed in order to start-up and operate the farm (Regulatory and Policy Issues).

It should also describe the approach that was taken in developing the operating strategy.

CROP MANAGEMENT

Crop management for a farm involves maximizing the food crops that can be produced on a piece of land to meet the objectives of the marketing strategy, in terms of the type, amount, and quality of crops that are to be produced. This involves an understanding of both the approach that will be used to produce the crops and the schedule for planting and harvesting the crops.

Discuss your approach to crop production including the specific method to be used such as vertical gardens, raised beds, surface planting, hydroponics, aquaponics, cold houses, or green houses.

Consider the following questions:

- How will you produce your crops?
- Will you use cold houses, hot houses, vertical gardens, raised beds, tilling natural soil, or some combination?
- Will your crops be produced organically?
- Do you intend to be certified as an organic producer?
- What will be accomplished in-house or purchased?

- Will existing soil be used and will actions be need to improve existing soil conditions such as pH, organic content, nitrogen (N), phosphorus (P), and potassium (K)?
- Will compost or mulch be produced on your farm or purchased?
- Will seedlings be produced on your farm or purchased?
- What production management alternatives are going to be implemented for issues such as weed, pest, and disease control, soil fertility, crop rotation, tillage, water supply and irrigation, seed and plant selection, waste handling and disposal, and crop quality control?
- How will plantings be made to achieve the required crop harvest to meet the marketing strategy (e.g., overplanting)?
- Will you be planting and harvesting during multiple seasons, such as spring, summer, fall, and/or winter?
- How will your planting and harvesting schedules change over the first five years of production (e.g., crop rotation)?

Use *Worksheet # 15 (Crop Management)* to document information about your approach to production management. Use *Worksheet # 16 (Planting and Harvesting Schedules)* to evaluate your approach to planting and harvesting. Use *Worksheet #17 (Farm Planning)* to assist in estimating the operating expense for the farm.

YIELD

Discuss the estimate for the amount of crops that can be repeatedly produced (e.g., pounds of produce per month for each market segment and crop type) given the crop management approach, property size, and available resources. The output should be estimated for the first five years of operation. You may also want to estimate a high and low case output for purposes of evaluating the range of potential output against the objectives of the marketing strategy. These output projections should be consistent with your plans for the growth of the business. Describe your growth plans.

Use *Worksheet # 18 (Yield)* to document information about the farm capacity and size. Refer to data from *Worksheet #17 (Farm Planning)* to assist in estimating the size and capacity of the farm.

PHYSICAL RESOURCE NEEDS

Physical resources include land, buildings, and equipment necessary to produce and market your crops to meet the objectives of your marketing strategy. Discuss your physical resource needs and how they will be acquired. Describe the environmental factors related to the resources that will be needed to run the farm, such as water, electricity, and the impacts the farm may have on the environment (e.g., waste generation and disposal).

Consider the following questions:

- How much land will you need initially and within five years?
- How much land do you have available?
- Will you acquire land or lease land?
- Are there known or potential environmental issues on the property that will require assessment or cleanup on the property or require specific farming techniques to address?
- Has an environmental assessment and/or remedial action been conducted on the property?
- Are there physical conditions that present challenges to the use of the property (e.g., concrete foundations or floor slabs remaining, environmental restrains (e.g., land use restrictions)?
- What types of buildings and other structures are required initially and within five years?
- What resources will be needed for the farm, such as water, electricity, and waste disposal?

- What equipment, such as roto-tillers, tractors, vehicles, or refrigerators, is needed initially and within five years?
- What tools, such as rakes, hoes, and seed planters are needed initially and within five years?
- What supplies, such as fertilizers, mulch, compost, humus, seeds, crates, or labels, are needed?
- What type of irrigation system such as tile drains, drip zone irrigation or sprinkler system will be needed initially and within five years?
- How will resources be acquired?

Use *Worksheet # 19 (Physical Resources)* to document information about your physical resource needs.

HUMAN RESOURCE NEEDS

Describe the manpower needed to operate the farm. This should include management as well as farm labor. Estimates of the number and types of workers needed can be made by identifying the specific tasks that will be required on a daily basis on the farm, including administrative and management responsibilities, and estimating the number of hours per month for each task. These tasks can be grouped by skill or experience and the total number of hours for each group estimated. As an example, tasks can be grouped into marketing, operating, administrative, and finance.

Consider the following questions:

- What are the workforce needs for the first three to five years?
- What types of positions will be created for the farm?
- How many workers will be required for each position?
- What skills or experience will be required for each position?
- Will training be required or provided?
- Considering the number and types of workers needed, will the workforce consist of volunteers, part-time workers, full-time workers, third party services, or some combination?
- How will workers be compensated?
- What are the typical ranges for salaries for each position (e.g., $/hour, $/year)?
- Will benefits, such as vacation or medical coverage, be provided?

Use *Worksheet # 20 (Manpower Needs)* and *Worksheet # 21 (Workforce Needs)* to document information about workforce needs.

REGULATION AND POLICY

Operating a farm business will require a number of state or local zoning, permitting, licensing, and other regulatory issues be addressed. These regulatory requirements could have a significant impact on your production and operating plans, as well as on start-up costs. To minimize the impacts and properly plan production activities, identify the types of permits, licenses, or regulations and associated fees required to start up and conduct the business. Describe the political or legal factors that will influence or limit your activities. Your business must operate within governmental and regulatory requirements, such as zoning, planning and building requirements, waste management requirements, and sales and other tax requirements.

Consider the following questions:

- Are there political or legal factors that will influence or limit your activities?
- What regulatory requirements exist, such as conditional use permits, waste handling and disposal requirements or permits, health and safety plans and permits, building permits and inspection requirements, environmental permits, business licenses, and food handlers' licenses?

- Are there regulatory requirements or industry standards for handling, storing, packaging, and distributing the products?
- What conditions or issues are associated with each regulatory requirement?
- Can you meet each regulatory requirement?
- What fees are associated with the identified permits, licenses, or regulations?

Use *Worksheet # 22 (Regulation and Policy)* to document information about your approach to regulations and policies.

Financial Strategy

The financial strategy is divided into seven sections:
- Introduction.
- Expenses.
- Income.
- Profit and Loss.
- Fixed Assets.
- Funding Requirements.
- Risk Management.

Urban Oaks Farm, New Britain, Connecticut

INTRODUCTION

The introduction to the Financial Strategy summarizes for the reader:

- The estimated expenses for start-up and operation of the farm (Expenses).
- The projected income for the farm (Income).
- The projected profitability of the farm (Profitability).
- The anticipated fixed assets (Fixed Assets).
- The potential source of funding (Funding).
- The potential risks to the successful operation of the farm (Risk Management).

It should also describe the approach that was taken in developing the financial strategy.

EXPENSES

Develop a five-year projection for the annual expenses for the farm including adjustments for inflation using information such as the consumer price index (www.bls.gov/cpi/). The expenses should include the marketing expenses, operating expenses, and human resource expenses discussed in the marketing, operating, and human resource strategy sections of this business plan handbook. Expenses should also include administrative expenses related to the administration and management of the farm and one-time or initial start-up expenses, such as initial operating expenses, site preparation, environmental investigations, and remedial actions not treated or included as part of fixed asset costs. Discuss any assumptions used to develop the estimated expenses.

Use *Worksheet # 23 (Expenses)* to calculate and document the annual expenses.

INCOME

Develop a five-year projection for the annual income for the farm. The income should include receipts from the sales of produce and other products from the farm, less any loss associated with spoilage or product which cannot be sold. It should also include income from grants, donations, rent, or other sources which are anticipated on an annual basis to cover operating expenses. It is helpful to break down projected sales income by market segment to identify the contribution to income and evaluate the performance of each market segment. Identify any assumptions that were used to estimate the income.

Consider the following questions:

- For sources of income other than sales receipts, what are the sources of funding?
- What is the anticipated amount of funding that will be obtained from each source?
- What, if any, are the limitations on the use of the funding?

Use *Worksheet # 24 (Income)* to calculate and document the annual income.

PROFIT AND LOSS

Develop a five-year projection for the annual profit or loss for the farm. The annual profit or loss is the difference between the estimated annual expense and the estimated annual income.

Use *Worksheet # 25 (Profit and Loss)* to calculate and document the annual profit or loss.

FIXED ASSETS

Develop a five-year projection for the fixed assets that will require initial purchase or construction costs. Fixed assets normally include items such as land and buildings, motor vehicles, furniture, office equipment, computers, fixtures and fittings, and plant and machinery. These are items that are normally depreciated over time for tax purposes. Discuss any assumptions that were used to estimate the fixed asset costs.

Use *Worksheet # 26 (Fixed Assets)* to calculate and document the fixed assets and estimated costs to purchase and install.

FUNDING REQUIREMENTS

Describe the sources and amount of funding (capital) required to purchase and install the fixed assets needed to start up the farm and achieve the five-year goals of the business plan. Discuss the plans for obtaining the needed funding for the farm. Donations of equipment, such as vertical gardens or hoop houses, should be discussed along with the value associated with the donation. Any associated expenses should be included in the projected expenses for the farm (See Worksheet # 23).

Consider the following questions:

- What are the sources or potential sources of the funding?
- How much is needed?
- Will some or all of the capital requirements be financed?
- Are there specific limitations on the funding?
- What are the critical assumptions concerning the funding?
- What is the timing of the funding and how will it impact the achievement of the business plan?
- Are there any expenses associated with obtaining financing or funding, such as consulting expenses, filing fees, insurance?
- Is some of the funding going to be achieved through donations of equipment, buildings, or other fixed assets?

Use *Worksheet # 27 (Funding)* to calculate and document the sources of funding, the anticipated amount of funding that will be obtained from each source, and what, if any, are the limitations on the use of the funding. Use *Worksheet # 28 (Funding Information)* to document information concerning the funding needs and sources.

RISK MANAGEMENT

Identify and evaluate potential risks that can impact the financial strategy and the success of the business plan.

Consider the following questions:

- What are the potential risks that may need to be managed, such as production risks related to failure of a crop or unexpected low yield or environmental risks such as restrictions on land use?
- What are the marketing risks related to unexpected competitive actions, such as lower than expected competitor pricing?
- What are the financial risks related to loss of funding sources or low sales volume, or labor issues related to labor injuries or loss of the farm manager?
- How likely are the risks to occur?
- What can be done or what is planned to minimize these potential risks if they occur?
- What are the potential impacts on the financial strategy if there were changes in the assumptions for sales or production?

Use *Worksheet # 29 (Risk Management)* to document information on the potential risks that can impact the financial strategy.

Executive Summary

With the completion of the marketing, operating, and financial strategies, the details of the business plan are essentially complete. To finalize the business plan, an executive summary is developed. While the executive summary is the first section of your business plan, it is typically the last section to be written. The executive summary is a one or two page synopsis of your business plan that describes the plan and highlights the significant information presented in the plan.

The executive summary should provide a brief overview of the farm's:

- Product(s) or service(s).
- Target market(s) and marketing and sales plan.
- Development plan.
- Operating plan.
- Management structure and key personnel.
- Financial plan.

It is important to consider that the executive summary may be useful as a standalone summary of the business plan. The executive summary, therefore, should be written as a standalone document so that the summary, by itself, provides sufficient information for a reader to understand the business.

Appendices

Appendix A: List of Provided Worksheets

	Worksheet	Purpose	Where to Find It
1	Before You Begin	Document your reasons, expertise and resource needs.	Urban Farm Business Plan-Worksheets (MS Word)
2	Introduction	Document the information to include in the Business Plan introduction.	Urban Farm Business Plan-Worksheets (MS Word)
3	Vision	Document the information to include in the Business Plan vision statement.	Urban Farm Business Plan-Worksheets (MS Word)
4	Mission	Document the information to include in the Business Plan mission statement.	Urban Farm Business Plan-Worksheets (MS Word)
5	Goals	Document the information to include in the Business Plan goal discussion.	Urban Farm Business Plan-Worksheets (MS Word)
6	Organization & Management	Document the information about the organization & management of your business.	Urban Farm Business Plan-Worksheets (MS Word)
7	Market Analysis	Document the information to include in the market section.	Urban Farm Business Plan-Worksheets (MS Word)
8	Market Segments	Document the information about customers and market segments (complete one worksheet for each market segment).	Urban Farm Business Plan-Worksheets (MS Word)
9	Product	Document the information about your product (complete one worksheet for each market segment).	Urban Farm Business Plan-Worksheets (MS Word)
10	Distribution	Document the information about your approach to storage and distribution (complete one worksheet for each market segment).	Urban Farm Business Plan-Worksheets (MS Word)
11	Pricing	Document the information about your approach to pricing (complete one worksheet for each market segment).	Urban Farm Business Plan-Worksheets (MS Word)
12	Sales Volume	Document the information about potential sales volumes.	Urban Farm Business Plan-Worksheets (MS Word)
13	Competition	Document the information about competitors (complete one worksheet for each market segment).	Urban Farm Business Plan-Worksheets (MS Word)
14	Promotion	Document the information about your approach to promotion (complete one worksheet for each market segment).	Urban Farm Business Plan-Worksheets (MS Word)
15	Crop Management	Document the information about your approach to production management.	Urban Farm Business Plan-Worksheets (MS Word)
16	Planting & Harvesting Schedules	Evaluate approach to planting and harvesting.	Urban Farm Business Plan-Worksheets (MS Word)
17	Farm Planning	Assist in estimating the operating expense for the farm and size and capacity of the farm.	Urban Farm Business Plan-Worksheets (MS Excel)

	Worksheet	Purpose	Where to Find It
18	Yield	Document the information about farm capacity and size.	Urban Farm Business Plan-Worksheets (MS Word)
19	Physical Resources	Document the information about the physical resource needs.	Urban Farm Business Plan-Worksheets (MS Word)
20	Manpower Needs	Document the information about workforce needs.	Urban Farm Business Plan-Worksheets (MS Word)
21	Workforce Needs	Document the information about workforce needs.	Urban Farm Business Plan-Worksheets (MS Word)
22	Regulation & Policy	Document the information about your approach to regulations and policies.	Urban Farm Business Plan-Worksheets (MS Word)
23	Expenses	Calculate and document annual expenses.	Urban Farm Business Plan-Worksheets (MS Excel)
24	Income	Calculate and document the annual income.	Urban Farm Business Plan-Worksheets (MS Excel)
25	Profit & Loss	Calculate and document the annual profit or loss.	Urban Farm Business Plan-Worksheets (MS Excel)
26	Fixed Assets	Calculate and document the fixed assets and estimated costs to purchase and install.	Urban Farm Business Plan-Worksheets (MS Excel)
27	Funding	Calculate and document the sources of funding, the anticipated amount of funding that will be obtained from each source, and what, if any, are the limitations on the use of the funding.	Urban Farm Business Plan-Worksheets (MS Excel)
28	Funding Information	Document the information concerning the funding needs and sources.	Urban Farm Business Plan-Worksheets (MS Word)
29	Risk Management	Document the information about the potential risks that can impact the financial strategy.	Urban Farm Business Plan-Worksheets (MS Word)

Appendix B: Example Worksheets

The following example worksheets are provided to demonstrate the type of specific information that should be collected in order to develop a business plan. The information provided in the example worksheets is for a <u>hypothetical site and project scenario</u>. The data presented in the example worksheets demonstrate how information flows from one worksheet to another and does not necessarily reflect any particular project assumptions. When inputting data into the blank worksheets, care should be taken to ensure data inputs reflect individual urban farm assumptions.

Example Worksheet # 1 – Before You Begin

Think about the primary reasons why you want to start an urban farm and the expertise and resources needed to develop the business plan.

What are your primary reasons for starting an urban farm?
Place an abandoned industrial property into an economically viable and accessible source of fresh locally grown fruits and vegetables to the residents, businesses, and institutions within the community.   Provide job training and educational opportunities to the surrounding community.
What expertise is needed on your planning team?
Marketing expertise to evaluate and identify the markets and products that should be the focus of the growing center.   Operating and production expertise to evaluate and identify the growing approaches, requirement and facility requirements, and manpower needs.   Environmental expertise to evaluate impacts of property environmental condition and appropriate actions.   Developing sources of funding and evaluating operating expense and income requirements.
What resources will be needed to develop the business plan?
Consulting support to guide the drafting of the business plan, develop a marketing analysis and recommendation on markets and products.   Support from the *Nonprofit Food Group X* and *Community-based Group Y* to develop the operating strategy.   Funding for consulting requirements.
What values do you bring to this business that will help you define the success of the business?
Importance of food choices, healthy diets and lifestyles, and nutrition education.   Foster a sense of community by reconnecting people with locally grown foods.   Benefit public health and the environmental by cleaning up brownfields properties.   Develop sustainable reuses support community economic, social, and environmental goals by utilizing operation and production techniques that minimize pollution and conserve resources and providing opportunities for job training and education.   Provide affordable fresh fruits and vegetables.

Example Worksheet # 2 – Introduction

The introduction describes the purpose of the business plan and the key issues addressed by the plan.

What is the purpose of the business plan?
Outline the approach for the development, operation, and funding of the growing center. The business plan will also serve as a planning tool for the longer-term growth of the growing center and provide information to potential sources of funding for the development and operation of the growing center.
What information is contained in the business plan?
The business plan outlines the strategy for producing and marketing fresh fruits and vegetables within the area around the growing center. It describes the market to be targeted, the crops to be produced, the method of production, manpower needs and strategies for funding the development and operation of the growing center.
How was the business plan developed?
The business plan was developed with the help of the business planning team, students and professors from the University of Town X, and consultants funded by EPA and other sources.
Who are the members of the business planning team?
[Name] – Town X Community Development Corporation *[Name] – County Y Improvement Corporation* *[Name] – County Y Improvement Corporation* *[Name] – Assets Town X* *[Name] – Private Enterprises* *[Name] – The Collaborative Inc.* *[Name] – University of Town X*
What are the potential risks to the successful start up of the farm?
Funding for the development and expansion of the growing center. Sufficient volunteers and community support to construct and operate the facility. Crop yield and quality along with the timing of achieving consistent, viable, and marketable crops. Insufficient income and the need for funding to off-set the expenses during the first three to five years.

Example Worksheet # 3 – Vision

The vision statement is an inspirational statement that describes your vision for the future of the farm and how your values will be incorporated into your farm.

What economic, environmental, or community values are important to the success of the farm?
Economically viable source of fresh locally grown fruits and vegetables and related products to our community.   Productive reuse of abandoned properties, local jobs, and job training.   Benefit public health and the environment by cleaning up and utilizing operation and production techniques that minimize pollution and conserve resources.   Providing nutrition education and job training.

What products or services (in a general sense) do you expect to provide?
Fresh fruits and vegetables.   Job training.   Nutrition education.

Who are your target customers?
Members of the community surrounding the growing center including residents and commercial food business such as restaurants and community meal services.

What customer or market needs will your business address?
Provide fresh fruits and vegetables to residents that do not have easy access to these products or the economic means to purchase these products.   Provided locally grown fresh fruit and vegetables to restaurants in the community.

What do you expect the business to look like in the future?
Growing and marketing fruits and vegetables to the residents and business in the community utilizing organic and sustainable production methods generating sufficient income to off-set expenses.

How do you expect the business to be perceived by the community and customers in the future?
Community asset that provides not only fresh fruits and vegetables, but education, job training and a source of pride for the community. It is anticipated that the community will develop a sense of ownership in the operation and success of the growing center through volunteer efforts and purchase of its products. It is also anticipated that restaurants and other business will prefer products grown at the growing center and proudly advertise the growing center as the source of those products. In addition, it is hoped that the growing center will be a model for similar operations within the Town X area and other areas of the country.

Example Worksheet # 4 – Mission

The mission statement is a simple statement that communicates the fundamental purpose and expectations for the farm to customers and others outside of the business.

What is the overall purpose of your farm?
Promote the production and purchase of locally grown foods and to demonstrate the viability and sustainability of urban food production and commerce and its role as an integral part of the community landscape.
What is the overall goal of your farm?
Provide the community with access to affordable fresh produce, jobs and job training, and education on growing and preserving fresh produce and improved health through better diet.
What do you want your business to be known for in the future?
Quality locally grown fresh fruit and vegetables.   A source of education, training and community pride.
To who do you want the mission statement to communicate?
The social and economic benefits of urban farming and the viability and sustainability of such efforts.

Example Worksheet # 5 – Goals

The goals describe what is to be achieved by the business in the future.

What will the business market?
The business will market fresh fruits and vegetables consistent with the cultural and dietary needs of the community.
How will the business operate?
The business will operate under the umbrella of the Town X CDC. It is expected that within the first five years that the facility will be producing crops over in three growing seasons – spring, summer, fall. Crop production will be accomplished using vertical gardens and hoop houses with raised growing beds. Marketing will be through a farm stand on the property and direct marketing to customers.
Who will be involved in operations?
The growing center will be managed by an experience farm manager and be staffed by students and community volunteers.
What income or earnings are expected from the business?
The growing center is expected to operate at a loss until the fifth year of operation, Income and expenses of approximately $100,000 are expected by the fifth year of operation.
What are the short-term goals (1-5 years)?
Engage the community in the growing center operations and production.   Construct the initial hoop house and install the vertical gardens with initial crops in summer 2011.   Construct the farm stand and training center.   Bring the facility to its full anticipated production capacity consisting of four hoop houses, vertical gardens, a farm stand, a training center, and support buildings.   Sales will be to both local residents, transient residents at the farm stand, and to local food service business.

Example Worksheet # 5 – Goals

What are the long-term goals (greater than 5 years)?

Expand the market to larger food service businesses such as nursing homes, school lunch programs and expand the facility to meet the needs of these additional markets. This would require the acquisition of additional property in the area of the growing center.

Incorporate aquaponics into the production operations.

Add composting operations.

Additional products such as jams, salsas, and packaged salad mixes.

The growing center will be able to off-set operating expenses with annual income and generate an annual profit.

What goals are most important to achieving success in the business?

Engaging the community in the operation and production of the growing center. Volunteer workers are an important component of the construction and initial operation of the facility.

Bringing the facility up to full production within the first five years.

What short-term goals are necessary for the long term success of the business?

Developing the market through sales.

Engaging the community in the growing center operations and production.

What is the priority of the goals?

1) Engage the community in the growing center operations and production.

2) Construct the initial hoop house and install the vertical gardens with initial crops in summer 2011.

3) Construct the farm stand and training center.

4) Sales will be to both local residents, transient residents at the farm stand, and to local food service business.

5) Bring the facility to its full anticipated production capacity consisting of four hoop houses, vertical gardens, a farm stand, a training center, and support buildings.

Example Worksheet # 6 – Organization and Management

Describe how the business will be organized and who will manage the business.

How will the business be organized?
The growing center will be operated by the Town X Community Development Corporation (CDC). The facility will be managed by a farm manager employed by the Town X CDC reporting to the Executive director. Administrative, financial, and legal support will be provided by existing Town X CDC staff.
What is the ownership structure of the business?
The growing center will be owned by the Town X CDC.
Will there be an overseeing board or board of directors? Who will be on it? What will their roles be in the business? Will there be compensation for these directors?
The operation of the growing center will be overseen by the Executive Director and Board of the Town X CDC.
How will the business management be organized? A simple organization chart may be useful to explain the organization.
A farm manager will manage the day-to-day operations of the farm. Staff and volunteer workers will report to the farm manager. The farm manager will report to the Executive Director of the Town X CDC. Administrative activities of the farm will be managed by the Executive Director of the Town X CDC.
Who will be the key managers who will run the business?
The key managers are the farm manager and the Executive Director of the Town X CDC.
What unique skills do the key managers bring to the business?
The farm manager brings a background in agriculture, crop, and farm management. The Executive Director of the Town X CDC provides administrative, marketing, and financial experience.
What will be the duties and responsibilities of the key managers?
The farm manager will manage the day-to-day operations of the farm. Staff and volunteer workers will report to the farm manager. The farm manager will report to the Executive Director of the Town X CDC. Administrative activities of the farm will be managed by the Executive Director of the Town X CDC.
How will the key managers be compensated?
The farm manager will be paid and hourly rate with certain benefits. The Executive Director will perform the responsibilities associated with the growing center as part of the Executive Director position.

Example Worksheet # 7 – Market Analysis

The market analysis describes the general environment in which your business will be operating.

What are the economic factors that affect a potential customer's purchasing power and spending?
Low- to moderate-income neighborhood surrounding the growing center that is currently underserved by full service grocery stores. Households have lower spending power than those in the greater County Y area.
What are the demographic factors that describe who potential customers are, where they are, and how many are likely to buy your product?
The site neighborhood is bounded by major area east-west and north-south corridors that experience significant traffic counts. The growing center is strategically located between downtown Town X and the University of Town X campus with the potential to capture vehicular traffic from non-residents. The growing center's proximity to large concentrations of consumers facilitates transportation and delivery of product. Per capita consumption of fresh fruits and vegetables has increased steadily between 1980 and 2001, and is projected to continue to increase through 2020. According to the United States Department of Agriculture's Agricultural Marketing Resource Center (2004), between 1980 and 2001, per capita consumption of fresh fruits increased by 19% and consumption of vegetables (including potatoes) increased by 29%. The USDA forecasts that the trend toward increased consumption of fresh fruits and vegetables will continue. Per capita expenditures on fruits and vegetables are expected to have the highest increases among all types of foods through 2020.
What are the social and cultural factors related to the basic values, perceptions, preferences, and behaviors of your potential customers?
There is a growing desire among the community for easily accessible and reasonably priced fresh fruits and vegetables consistent with the cultural make-up of the community.
What voids in the market will be filled by your farm?
Availability of locally grown organically grown fruits and vegetables for the direct to consumer and wholesale markets within an approximate 2-mile radius of the growing center.

Example Worksheet # 8 – Market Segments

Divide the larger target market into submarkets (market segments), such as direct marketing to individual households or business-to-business marketing. Describe the characteristics of each market segment. Complete a worksheet for each market segment.

Market Segment: Retail, Direct to Consumer
What is the size and geographic location?
Primary market area includes downtown and neighborhoods within approximately 2.0 miles of the growing center.
What characteristics (demographics) define the target customers?
The market area consists of low- to moderate income with lower-than-average and educational attainment levels.
What are the attributes of the market segment related to personality, values, attitudes, interests, or lifestyles?
Types of crops to be grown. Access to and ease of purchase. Social and economic impact on the immediate neighborhood.
What are the needs and preferences of the market segment?
Easily accessible and reasonably priced fresh fruits and vegetables consistent with the cultural make-up of the community.
What are the trends and/or market conditions for each market segment?
Per capita consumption of fresh fruits and vegetables has increased steadily between 1980 and 2001, and is projected to continue to increase through 2020. Growing consumer preferences for fresh, organic, local produce is driving a greater diversity of fruit and vegetable offerings in grocery stores, and a strong increase in farmers markets. Farm-to-consumer sales are a relatively small share of the overall "food consumed at home" market (1.1% in 2009).
What product will appeal to each market segment?
Fresh, affordable and healthy fruits and vegetables.

Example Worksheet # 8 – Market Segments

Market Segment: Retail, Direct to Consumer
What motivates buying decisions in each market segment?
Mobility – ability to travel to grocery store. Easy access to the produce. Reasonably priced (affordable) produce. Locally produced quality produce.
What evidence is there that potential customers in each market segment want the product?
In addition to national studies that show an increasing trend in the purchase of organic, fresh produce, surveys of 173 local residents conducted by the Toledo CDC indicate that residents in the area of the growing center are interested in purchasing locally grown fruits and vegetables.

Market Segment: Wholesale, Direct to Restaurants
What is the size and geographic location?
Primary market area includes restaurants downtown and neighborhoods within approximately 2.0 miles of the growing center.
What characteristics (demographics) define the target customers?
Experienced chefs with knowledge of the nutritional values of fruits and vegetables.
What are the attributes of the market segment related to personality, values, attitudes, interests, or lifestyles?
Types of crops to be grown. Require high quality and appearance. Looking for cost effective product or sufficient quality and appearance to obtain premium price for fresh, organic fruits and vegetables.
What are the needs and preferences of the market segment?
Competitively priced fresh fruits and vegetables. Availability to meet demand. Fruits and vegetables compatible with their menus.

Example Worksheet # 8 – Market Segments

Market Segment: Wholesale, Direct to Restaurants
What are the trends and/or market conditions for each market segment?
Per capita consumption of fresh fruits and vegetables has increased steadily between 1980 and 2001, and is projected to continue to increase through 2020. Growing consumer preferences for fresh, organic, local produce is driving a greater diversity of fruit and vegetable offerings in grocery stores, and a strong increase in farmers markets. Buying fresh, local foods is one of the strongest trends among today's chefs, listed among the top 10 trends of 2010 in the American Restaurant Association's survey of 1,800 U.S. chefs.
What product will appeal to each market segment?
Fresh, affordable and healthy fruits and vegetables.
What motivates buying decisions in each market segment?
Reasonably priced produce. Quality and appearance. Compatibility with menu. Consistent supply.
What evidence is there that potential customers in each market segment want the product?
Chefs in the Town X area who currently purchase fresh produce from local farms responded positively to the proposed Town X Growing Center concept. Several noted that they would be interested in purchasing produce from the Town X Growing Center, once established.

Example Worksheet # 9 – Products

Describe the products to be offered and how they will compete in each market segment.
Complete a worksheet for each market segment.

Market Segment: Retail, Direct to Consumer
What products will be offered?
Herbs – (basil, sage, dill, parsley, rosemary). Leaf greens (collard, turnip). Salad greens. Broccoli. Cucumbers. Cabbage. Spinach. Berries (strawberries, raspberries, blackberries). Potatoes (Longer term in years three to five). Tilapia and other fish (Longer term based on implementation of aquaponics in year's three to five). Other crops will be added based on demand and growing capabilities.
What is the product availability (seasonal offerings)?
What specific product characteristics meet the needs of the market segment?
Fresh. Locally grown. Appearance. Accessibility.
How are your products unique?
Grown locally at a facility supported by the community. Provide job training and nutritional education to the community. Restore a former abandoned industrial property to a productive use.
Why would a customer prefer your product to a competitor's?
The growing center will cater to the needs of the local community with respect to crop planning and community quality of life. Support job training and local education.

Example Worksheet # 9 – Products

Market Segment: Wholesale, Direct to Restaurants

What products will be offered?

Herbs – (basil, sage, dill, parsley, rosemary).
Baby vegetables (carrots and beets).
Salad greens.
Broccoli.
Cucumbers.
Spinach.
Berries (strawberries, raspberries).
Other crops will be added based on demand and growing capabilities.

What is the product availability (seasonal offerings)?

What specific product characteristics meet the needs of the market segment?

Fresh.
Locally grown.
Appearance.
Cost.

How are your products unique?

Grown locally at a facility supported by the community.

Why would a customer prefer your product to a competitor's?

The growing center will cater to the needs of the local community with respect to crop planning and community quality of life.

Support job training and local education.

Example Worksheet # 10 – Distribution

Describe how the product is planned to be distributed and how the product will get to each market segment. Complete a worksheet for each market segment.

Market Segment: Retail, Direct to Consumer

Will the product be pre-packaged? How will the product be packaged?

The product will be sold by the piece to consumers at the farm stand on the growing center or at local farmers markets. Fruits and vegetables shipped off the growing center will be packaged in cartons, crates or bags, as appropriate for the specific fruit or vegetable.

Will the product be stored prior to sale? How will the product be stored?

Fruits and vegetables will not be stored for extended periods of time at the growing center; however, harvested fruits and vegetables will be stored within the storage building or hoop house on the growing center property until sold or donated. Fruits and vegetables that cannot be sold within two to three days of harvest will be donated to local food service providers for the homeless or elderly.

How will the product be distributed (farm stand, deliveries)?

Farm stand on the growing center property.

Community group volunteers will distribute to local churches, senior centers, and youth groups.

Produce will be hauled to select Town X area farmers markets on a weekly or bi-weekly basis.

How will product quality be maintained during storage and distribution?

As noted previously, fruits and vegetables will not be stored for long periods of time. Harvested crops will be placed in cartons or crates as appropriate for the particular fruit or vegetable and stored within the storage building or hoop house on the growing center property.

Why is the selected distribution approach best for the market segment?

The product of the growing center is fresh fruits and vegetables. Long term storage of the crops will not meet this objective or objectives related to quality and appearance.

How will your business gain access to the market segment and distribution channels?

A network of community group volunteers who focus on churches, senior centers, youth and family centers.

Events and tasting at the growing center and at area farmers markets.

How often will the product be made available to customers in each marketing segment (deliveries, days and hours of operation)?

Once or twice a week to senior groups, schools, and churches.

Example Worksheet # 10 – Distribution

Market Segment: Wholesale, Direct to Restaurants
Will the product be pre-packaged? How will the product be packaged?
The product will be sold by the piece to chefs at the farm stand on the growing center or at local farmers markets. Fruits and vegetables shipped off the growing center will be packaged in cartons, crates or bags, as appropriate for the specific fruit or vegetable.
Will the product be stored prior to sale? How will the product be stored?
Fruits and vegetables will not be stored for extended periods of time at the growing center; however, harvested fruits and vegetables will be stored within the storage building or hoop house on the growing center property until sold or donated. Fruits and vegetables that cannot be sold within two to three days of harvest will be donated to local food service providers for the homeless or elderly.
How will the product be distributed (farm stand, deliveries)?
Farm stand on the growing center property. Community group volunteers will distribute to local restaurants.
How will product quality be maintained during storage and distribution?
Fruits and vegetables will not be stored for long periods of time. Harvested crops will be placed in cartons or crates as appropriate for the particular fruit or vegetable and stored within the storage building or hoop house on the growing center property.
Why is the selected distribution approach best for the market segment?
The product of the growing center is fresh fruits and vegetables. Long term storage of the crops will not meet this objective or objectives related to quality and appearance.
How will your business gain access to the market segment and distribution channels?
A network of community group volunteers who will make direct contact with chefs at local restaurants. Events and tasting at the growing center and at area farmers markets.
How often will the product be made available to customers in each marketing segment (deliveries, days and hours of operation)?
Deliveries will be based on the needs of the restaurant; however, it is anticipated that deliveries, where required, will be two to three times per week.

Example Worksheet # 11 – Pricing

Describe the pricing strategy for each market segment and why it will be effective with the target customer in the market segment. Pricing is based on prevailing market pricing and costs of producing and distributing the product. Complete a worksheet for each market segment.

Market Segment: Retail, Direct to Consumer

What are the prevailing market prices for similar products?

Market prices vary depending on season and crop yield.

What is the likely ability of your business to set prices?

The growing center has substantial opportunity for setting prices. At the farm stand on the growing center, pricing can reflect the lower overhead and lack of distribution costs resulting in lower that competition pricing. At farmer's markets, pricing can be competitive with the competition. In addition, the growing center has the opportunity to provide fresh fruits and vegetables to neighbors of the growing center in exchange for volunteer work at the center.

What is the sensitivity of demand to price?

For the primary market of residents living within a two-mile radius of the growing center, price will be a significant component of their decision to purchase fruits and vegetables from the growing center. Pricing will need to be within the limits of the low to middle income range of these residents.

How will the product be priced for each market segment?

The product will be priced based on competitive pricing and local economic means. In addition, pricing will be adjusted in exchange for volunteer labor and other activities to support the growing center.

How does your pricing strategy compare with the competition?

The growing center has an advantage in that it will have a lower overhead and distribution costs than many of its competitors. It also has the opportunity to provide "pick your own" pricing and pricing adjustments based on volunteer support.

What evidence is there that the target market will accept the price?

Surveys conducted by the Town X CDC indicate that if fresh fruits and vegetables can be provided at a cost equal to or less than the current sources of these items, that the community is likely to purchase their produce from the growing center.

Why will the selected pricing strategy be effective?

The pricing strategy is competitive and recognizes the economic requirements of the community.

Example Worksheet # 11 – Pricing

Market Segment: Wholesale, Direct to Restaurants
What are the prevailing market prices for similar products?
Market prices vary depending on season and crop yield. Below are estimates based on 2010 market wholesale prices: Herbs – $10.00 to $15.00 per pound. Baby vegetables – $4.00 - $5.00 per pound. Salad greens – romaine $1.50 per pound; butter bib $2.00 each. Broccoli – $0.67 - $1.00 per pound. Cucumbers – $0.65 per pound. Spinach – $1.75 per pound. Berries (strawberries – $2.75 - $3.50 per pound, raspberries – $5.00 per pint).
What is the likely ability of your business to set prices?
The growing center has substantial opportunity for setting prices; however, prices will need to be competitive with the wholesale market.
What is the sensitivity of demand to price?
Demand will be very sensitive to price; although there may be opportunity for a small premium based on the community basis of the growing center assuming a quality product.
How will the product be priced for each market segment?
The product will be priced based on the competition.
How does your pricing strategy compare with the competition?
The growing center has an advantage in that it will have a lower overhead and distribution costs than many of its competitors. It also has the opportunity to provide "pick your own" pricing and pricing adjustments based on volunteer support.
What evidence is there that the target market will accept the price?
The marketing analysis indicates that if consistent quality fresh fruits and vegetables can be provided at a cost equal to or less than the current sources of these items, that the restaurants are likely to purchase their produce from the growing center.
Why will the selected pricing strategy be effective?
The pricing strategy is competitive.

Example Worksheet # 12 – Sales Volume

Develop simple sales projections for each market segment using information about average product consumption, geographic location, and customer attributes, needs, and preferences. Complete a worksheet for each market segment.

Market Segment: Retail, Direct to Consumer
When and how long will the product be available for this market segment?
Initial crops will be available in the summer of 2011. It is planned to provide produce over three growing seasons (spring, summer, and fall).
What is the potential number of customers for each market segment?
Residents with a 2-mile radius of the growing center. Transient consumers. Consumers at local farmers markets.
What is the potential volume per customer for the market segment?
Volume per customer estimate not developed.
What is the potential sales volume for the market segment?
It is anticipated that total sales volume based on farm capacity will be approximately $27,000 in the fifth year of operation.
What assumptions were made about the market segment?
The primary, or target customer is residents of the surrounding low-income neighborhoods that have limited access to fresh fruits and vegetables. It is expected that sales to these customers will be made at the farm stand at the growing center, or at targeted locations such as churches, senior centers, youth centers and schools. Direct to customer sales will likely also be conducted from sales sites such as local farmers markets to a larger area within County Y competing regionally with a wide variety of grocers, farm stands and other retailers.
What research was conducted or referenced about the market segment?
A Market Analysis was conducted by Firm Z for the Town X CDC. Surveys of area residents were conducted by the Town X CDC.

Example Worksheet # 12 – Sales Volume

Market Segment: Wholesale, Direct to Restaurants
When and how long will the product be available for this market segment?
Initial crops for this market segment the third year of the growing center operation in order to achieve the quality, appearance and supply of product required by this market segment. It is planned to provide produce over three growing seasons (spring, summer, and fall).
What is the potential number of customers for each market segment?
The potential market is any restaurant within the downtown area and a 2-mile radius of the growing center. The State Regional 2010 Directory identifies over 30 restaurants and catering facilities that utilize locally grown produce.
What is the potential volume per customer for the market segment?
It is anticipated that total sales volume based on farm capacity will be approximately $20,000 in the fifth year of operation.
What is the potential sales volume for the market segment?
Volume per customer estimate not developed.
What assumptions were made about the market segment?
Chefs will be more likely to buy fresh produce produced in the immediate area of the restaurant. It is expected that sales to these customers will be made at the farm stand at the growing center and direct marketing to the restaurants.
What research was conducted or referenced about the market segment?
A Market Analysis was conducted by Firm Z for the Town X CDC including surveys of chefs in the market area.

Example Worksheet # 13 – Competition

Describe the competition for each market segment and how the business will be positioned to compete in each market segment. Complete a worksheet for each market segment.

Market Segment: Retail, Direct to Consumer
Who are the competitors for each market segment?
There is no direct retail competition in the immediate site neighborhood. Larger chain grocers such as Market A and Chain Grocery Store "S" are located on the northern fringe of the market area and there is a Chain Grocery Store "SL" located less than 0.5 miles north of the growing center at the corner of "L" and "M" Streets. Town X Farmers Market (downtown and suburban locations). Natural Food Co-op.
What are the advantages of your business in this market segment?
Location within the community with weak retail competition - Over 70% of the residents surveyed in the area of the growing center responded that if fresh local produce were available in their area, they would be very likely to purchase locally. The highest share of those who responded positively to this question responded that they would be most likely to purchase produce at a farmers market in the community. Produce that is local and organic; an accessible location; highly visible; community ties and neighborhood investment; established networks with community groups from the Town X CDC; at the source fruits and vegetables.
What are the disadvantages of your business in this market segment?
The convenience of shopping at larger grocery stores will compete with the growing center as shoppers may favor one stop shopping over fresh and local fruits and vegetables. Mobility of the residents within the PMA; Consumer Buying Patterns: Produce is not as "cost efficient" as fast food.
How will your business differentiate itself from your competitors? Why will customers switch to or select this business?
Community based business that not only provides fresh fruits and vegetables, but provides job training, nutritional education, and volunteer opportunities for the community. Community supported agriculture (CSA) approach will be implemented once the crop production reaches a critical mass sufficient to support this approach. Customers will frequent this facility because of its accessibility, convenience, quality product.

Example Worksheet # 13 – Competition

Market Segment: Wholesale, Direct to Restaurants

Who are the competitors for each market segment?

The growing center would compete with grocery stores, produce wholesalers and local farms for business with local restaurants.

Area growers include:
- Berry Farm, Town Y, USA (berries and berry products).
- "X" Farms, Town A, USA.
- "B" Farms, Town B, USA.
- "C" Greenhouse and Strawberry Farm, Town C, USA.
- "LK" Farm, Town C, USA.
- "MQ" Orchards, Town D, USA.
- "TMC" Farm, Town E, USA.
- "GT" Farms, Town D, USA (strawberries only).
- "Z" Farms, Town F, USA.

Area wholesale distributors of fresh local produce include*:
- "AP" & Sons & Daughter Too, Town X, USA.
- "C" Foods Inc., Town X, USA.
- "SO" Produce Company, Town X, USA.
- "S" Foods, Town X, USA.

What are the advantages of your business in this market segment?

Location within the community.

Produce that is local and organic.

An accessible location; highly visible.

Community ties and neighborhood investment.

At the source fruits and vegetables.

What are the disadvantages of your business in this market segment?

The convenience of purchasing from larger farms or wholesale suppliers.

Limited selection of fruits and vegetables.

New to the market segment.

How will your business differentiate itself from your competitors? Why will customers switch to or select this business?

Community based business that not only provides fresh fruits and vegetables, but provides job training, nutritional education, and volunteer opportunities for the community.

Customers will frequent this facility because of its accessibility, convenience, quality product, community support.

Example Worksheet # 14 – Promotion

Describe how the product will be sold and what will be communicated to customers in each market segment. Complete a worksheet for each market segment.

Market Segment: Retail, Direct to Consumer
How will your business gain access to the market segments?
Soliciting support and ownership by the community of the growing center in the surrounding neighborhood. Town X CDC contacts with local organizations, churches and other community groups. Erect signs visible from "D" Avenue as well as "D" Street to direct visitors to the growing center and on the fence surrounding the growing center. Community recruitment and volunteers for the development and operation of the growing center. Program participation: Supplemental Nutrition Assistance Program (SNAP), Women, Infants, and Children (WIC) supplemental nutrition program, and Farmer's Market Nutrition Program (FMNP). Reward volunteer groups with snacks and/or take-away such as a share of the crop.
What approach will you use for promotion?
During the first year, the surrounding neighborhood and interest organizations will be asked to participate in a number of promotions: tree planting, and opening ceremony, web promotions, database management, marketing communications and program participation. Contest to develop the logo for the growing center. Students and artists from the surrounding neighborhood will be asked to create the signs with materials donated to the Town X Growing Center from Habitat for Humanity or other local organizations. Competition for local artists and students could be coordinated by a local high school art teacher.
What message will you communicate to your potential customers?
Fresh fruits and vegetables locally grown within the community. Community volunteers needed and welcomed. Educational and job training opportunities. Encourage ownership in the growing center and its success within the community.
How often will customers be contacted through advertising and communications?
Regular (at least monthly) visits to local church groups, senior centers, youth centers and school classes to work and learn during the Town X Growing Center's first growing year.

Example Worksheet # 14 – Promotion

Market Segment: Wholesale, Direct to Restaurants
How will your business gain access to the market segments and distribution channels?
Direct contact with chefs at local restaurants. Requests by customers of restaurants that are also members of the community around the growing center.
What approach will you use for promotion?
Direct contact with chefs at local restaurants. Word of mouth by customers of restaurants that are also members of the community around the growing center. Advertising (e.g., fliers).
What message will you communicate to your potential customers?
Quality fresh fruits and vegetables locally grown within the community. Competitively priced. Consistent supply.
How often will customers be contacted through advertising and communications?
Regular (at least monthly) contacts or visits to area restaurants.

Example Worksheet # 15 – Crop Management

Production management for a farm involves maximizing the food crops that can be produced on a piece of land in order to meet the objectives of the marketing strategy, in terms of the type, amount, and quality of crops that are to be produced, and the profitability of those crops.

What approach will be used for crop production (native soil plantings, raised beds, aquaponics)?

Crops will be grown in four 30 feet wide by 96 feet long hoop houses. Each hoop house will contain 24 – 30 four feet wide by eight feet long raised planter beds. Vertical gardens will be used during the spring and summer growing seasons for berries. It is anticipated that one of the four hoop houses will include an aquaponics system to be utilized for both raising fish such as tilapia and vegetables.

In year one, a single hoop house along with vertical gardens will be installed with initial plantings in the spring. The second and third hoop houses will be erected during the first year for use in the second year. The fourth hoop house will be erected in the second year for use in the third year with the aquaponics production anticipated in the fourth or fifth year of operation using a portion or all of one of the fourth hoop house. The vertical gardens will be installed and plantings accomplished in spring of the first year.

Crop production techniques will be developed with the assistance of Town X Grows, the University of Town X, and the *Nonprofit Food Technology*.

In addition to crop production facilities, an 1800 square foot educational facility including a class room and rest rooms will be constructed on the site during the first year. In addition, a free standing farm stand will also be provided on the side with an enclosure added in the second year or third year.

Storage of tools and other equipment will be on shelves and benches constructed within the hoop houses until a storage shed is erected in the second year.

What crop management alternatives will be implemented (e.g., weed, pest and disease control)?

All crop production will use organic growing methods to meet the criteria of a certified organic crop production facility. Organic pest management practices will be implemented to develop and maintain healthy soils and strong plants that can withstand pests and encourage beneficial insects by creating environments that attract them. Crop selection will focus on biodiversity in the crops and crop varieties that are resistant to pests and diseases. Selected approved substances will be used when necessary.

How will soil fertility be addressed (e.g., enhance existing soils, compost, mulch, fertilizer)?

Organic materials such as cover crops, crop residues, and compost will be added to soils to build soil organic matter and improve the ability of the soil to supply nutrients to the plants. It is anticipated that composting will be conducted on the growing center.

What type of water supply (e.g., city water, well) and irrigation system will be used (e.g., tile drains, drip zone irrigation, sprinkler systems)?

Water is supplied by the municipal water system. Plant irrigation will initially be accomplished by hand watering using a water spigot, hose and nozzle. Once there is a better understanding of the quantities of water needed other methods of watering such as drip irrigation will be evaluated.

Will seeds or seedlings be used? How will seed and plant selection be accomplished?

Seeds and seedlings will be obtained from a combination of "BS" Farms, Town X Grows, and Town X Botanical Gardens. Seedlings will ultimately be developed at the Growing Center.

Example Worksheet # 15 – Crop Management

What waste handling and disposal will be required and how will it be accomplished?
Organic waste such as crop residues will be composted on the site. Recyclable materials such as plastics, paper, and cardboard will be recycled. Extra crops that are not sold will be donated to community food centers. Disposal wastes will be minimized.
What quality control measures will be needed?
Quality control will be needed for all aspects of crop production and harvesting. Quality control will need to address soil fertility, plant survival, and the quality and appearance of the crops.
How will security for the property, equipment, and crops be accomplished (e.g., fencing, cameras)?
The property is fenced around its perimeter. An access gate for vehicles to enter the site and walk gates for customers and workers to enter the site.
Identify any other crop management issues (itemize)?
No other issues are identified at this time.

Example Worksheet # 16 – Planting and Harvesting Schedule

Discuss your planting and harvesting schedules.

How will plantings be made to achieve the required crop harvest to meet the marketing strategy?

An aggressive operational plan focused on highly productive cropping systems including crop rotation, succession planting, intercropping, companion planting, and timing of plantings including removal of plants prior to full production capacity to allow for the start of a second crop to advance production of a crop. It is anticipated that several growing seasons will be necessary prior to identification of the most productive approach for maximum capacity.

What is your planting and harvesting schedule? Identify the year each crop will first be planted.

Crop	Year	Activity	Jan	Feb	Mar	Apr	May	Jun	Jul	Aug	Sep	Oct	Nov	Dec
Broccoli	1	Plant			X X									
		Harvest					X	X	X	X	X	X		
Leaf Greens	1	Plant		X	X X	X								
		Harvest				X	X	X	X	X	X	X	X	
Herbs	1	Plant				X	X	X	X					
		Harvest					X	X	X	X	X			
Cucumbers	1	Plant					X	X	X					
		Harvest						X	X	X	X			
Spinach	1	Plant			X	X								
		Harvest				X	X			X	X	X		
Cabbage	1	Plant		X	X X									
		Harvest					X	X	X	X				
Potatoes	3	Plant			X	X								
		Harvest					X	X	X	X				
Carrots	3	Plant		X X	X									
		Harvest				X	X	X	X	X	X	X	X	
Beets	3	Plant			X X	X								
		Harvest					X	X	X	X	X	X		
Strawberries	1	Plant			X X									
		Harvest				X	X	X						

Note: *Estimates are based on three seasons of production. These estimates are provided for evaluation purposes and need to be reviewed and updated by the Farm Manager based on actual crops and planting and harvest schedules.*

Example Worksheet # 17 – Farm Planning

Estimate the operating expense and size and capacity of the farm.

Business Name **Town X Growing Center**

Hoop House

Total Length	96	ft
Total Width	30	ft
Width of Row	1.5	ft
Footpath Area	30%	percent
Tool Storage Area	25	ft2
Composting Area	25	ft2
Other	50	ft2
TOTAL GROWING AREA	**1916**	**ft2**
TOTAL BED LENGTH	**1277**	**ft**

Growing Medium (For Raised Beds)

Depth	18	inches
TOTAL SOIL VOLUME	**958**	**yards**

Hoop House

Crop	Percent of Total Growing Area	Crops					Inputs			
		Distance Between Plants (ft)	Time to Maturity (from seed) (days)	Yield (per plant) (pounds)	Yield (per foot of row) (pounds)	Market Price (per pound) ($)	Seed/ Starter ($/plant)	Nutrients ($/ft2/day)	Pest Control ($/ft2/day)	Water ($/ft2/day)	TOTAL COST OF INPUTS ($/ft2/day)
Broccoli	15%	2.0	60	1.50	0.8	$ 1.69	$0.010	$0.001	$ 0.001	$ 0.001	$0.003
Leaf Greens	25%	0.5	45	0.38	0.8	$3.00	$0.010	$0.001	$0.001	$0.001	$0.003
Herbs	5%	0.3	60	0.02	0.1	$3.00	$0.010	$0.001	$0.001	$0.001	$ 0.004
Cucumbers	15%	1.0	45	1.20	1.2	$ 0.65	$0.010	$0.001	$0.001	$0.001	$0.003
Spinach	25%	0.3	45	0.13	0.4	$1.75	$0.010	$0.001	$0.001	$0.001	$0.004
Cabbage	15%	2.0	75	3.00	1.5	$0.69	$0.010	$0.001	$0.001	$0.001	$0.003

Total   100%

Example Worksheet # 17 – Farm Planning

Data Calculations and Outputs

Hoop House

Crop	Percent of Total Growing Area	Total Length of Row (ft)	Expected Annual Yield 3 Season (lbs)	Expected Annual Yield 4 Season (lbs)	Value of Annual Yield 3 Season	Value of Annual Yield 4 Season	Annual Cost of Inputs 3 Season	Annual Cost of Inputs 4 Season	Growing Seasons
Broccoli	15%	192	656	874	$1,108	$1,477	$243	$ 323	3
Leaf Greens	25%	319	1457	1943	$4,371	$5,828	$452	$602	3
Herbs	5%	64	15	19	$44	$58	$92	$122	3
Cucumbers	15%	192	1399	1865	$909	$1,212	$254	$338	3
Spinach	25%	319	777	1036	$1,360	$1,813	$481	$641	3
Cabbage	15%	192	1049	1399	$724	$965	$241	$322	3
	100%	**1277**			**$8,515**	**$11,354**	**$1,762**	**$2,349**	

Example Worksheet # 18– Yield (Size and Capacity)

Describe the production capacity and plans for future growth. Complete one worksheet for each market segment. Farm Planning worksheets are provided in Appendix B to assist in estimating the size and capacity of the farm. An electronic version is available, upon request.

What is the estimated output for each crop for this market segment during the first five years of production (e.g., pounds of produce per month)?					
Market Segment: Retail, Direct to Consumer					
Crop	Year 1	Year 2	Year 3	Year 4	Year 5
Expected Output					
Broccoli	656	1,345	1062	1316	1135
Leaf Greens	1,457	2,990	2124	2631	2271
Herbs	15	30	35	44	38
Cucumbers	1,399	2,870	2265	2807	2422
Spinach	777	1,595	1133	1403	1211
Cabbage	1049	2153	2549	3157	2725
Potatoes	0	0	1133	1403	1211
Carrots	0	0	944	1169	1009
Beets	0	0	1416	1754	1514
Strawberries	600	600	600	600	600
What are the plans for growth of the business for this market segment?					
Initial sales for this market will be through the onsite farm stand and local farmers markets. Growth in this market will be through increased crop production and variety and the establishment of a Community Supported Agriculture (CSA) approach for the farm. In addition, acceptance of Electronic Benefit Cards (EBT) cards and participation in resident assistance programs will also be pursued.					

Note: *Estimates are based on three seasons of production. These estimates are provided for evaluation purposes and need to be reviewed and updated by the Farm Manager based on actual crops and planting and harvest schedules. Strawberry production assumes 20 vertical units with five growing pots and four plants per pot.*

Example Worksheet # 18– Yield (Size and Capacity)

What is the estimated output for each crop for this market segment during the first five years of production (e.g., pounds of produce per month)?

Market Segment: Wholesale, Direct to Restaurants

Crop	Year 1	Year 2	Year 3	Year 4	Year 5
Expected Output (lbs)					
Broccoli	0	0	295	501	1,022
Leaf Greens	0	0	590	1,002	2,044
Herbs	0	0	10	17	34
Cucumbers	0	0	629	1,069	2,180
Spinach	0	0	315	535	1,090
Cabbage	0	0	315	535	1,090
Carrots	0	0	965	1,292	1,938
Beets	0	0	965	1,292	1,938
Strawberries	0	0	0	0	0

What are the plans for growth of the business for this market segment?

Entry into this market is not anticipated until crop production techniques and product quality objectives for this market segment have been achieved. This is expected in the third year of operation. Growth in this market segment will be achieved through direct marketing to local restaurants and expansion of the crop variety to meet the needs of this market.

Note: *Estimates are based on three seasons of production. These estimates are provided for evaluation purposes and need to be reviewed and updated by the Farm Manager based on actual crops and planting and harvest schedules.*

Example Worksheet # 19 – Physical Resources

Physical resources include land, buildings, and equipment necessary to produce and market your crops to meet the objectives of the marketing strategy. Describe your physical resource needs and how they will be acquired.

List the resources needed	Describe the physical resource and how it will be acquired. Describe any issues which may affect the use of or access to the resource (e.g., suspected or know environmental contamination on the property).
Land	
1646 Town X Avenue, Town X, USA.	Two plus acre former industrial property has been acquired by the Town X CDC. Environmental issues consistent with the former industrial use of the property were identified and environmental assessment and remediation activities conducted on the property. Approximately 60% of the property is covered by concrete associated with the floor and foundation of the former building located on the property. Soil on the property is not suitable for growing. The concrete pads must remain in place as a condition of the environmental remedial action.
Buildings	
Four 30 feet by 96 feet hoop houses. Educational facility (1800 square feet). Storage building.	Hoop houses will be purchased as a kit and erected on the site. Lumber and additional hardware will also be purchased. The educational facility and storage building will be designed for the specific purposed and constructed on site.
Other Structures	
Vertical gardens. Raised beds. Farm stand.	Vertical gardens have been donated by *Nonprofit Food Technology* and will be erected on the site. Lumber and other hardware for construction of the raised beds will be purchased. The farm stand will initially be an "open air" stand located on the property. An enclosed farm stand is anticipated in the fourth or fifth year of operation.

Example Worksheet # 19 – Physical Resources

Equipment	
No specific equipment has been identified for the initial years of operation.	Once crop production reaches the full capacity of the facility, it is anticipated that a vehicle may be needed to deliver product. This is not anticipated until at least the fifth year of operation.
Tools	
Gardening tools. Construction/maintenance tools.	Gardening tools include racks, shovels, hoses, spray nozzles. Tools will be obtained through donations or purchased as needed. Construction/maintenance tools include hand tools such as hammers, screw drivers, wrenches and power tools such as saws and drills. Tools will be obtained through donations or purchased as needed.
Supplies	
Soil. Compost.	Soil and compost will be needed initially to establish the raised beds and initiate crop production. Soil and compost will be obtained through donations or purchased as needed. Compost is anticipated to be produced on site in the future.
Utilities	
Water. Electric. Sewer. Natural gas.	Utilities will be purchased from local suppliers. Water lines with frost proof spigots will need to be run to each hoop hose and the vertical gardens as they are constructed. Electricity for lighting and weather proof electrical outlets will also need to be run to each hoop house and the vertical garden as they are constructed. Water, electric, sewer, and natural gas will need to be provided to the education facility and electricity will need to be provided to the storage shed and farm stand on the site as part of the building construction.
Other Resources (Itemize)?	
Composting facility.	The type of facility will be evaluated once anticipated production quality and productivity has been achieved and the amount of composted needed has been determined. In addition, a source of organic material other than crop residue generated on the site may be needed.

Example Worksheet # 20 – Manpower Needs

Identify the labor tasks and estimate the number of hours per week and weeks per year required for each task.

Task	Year 1 Hours/week	Year 1 Weeks/year	Year 1 Total	Year 2 Hours/week	Year 2 Weeks/year	Year 2 Total	Year 3 Hours/week	Year 3 Weeks/year	Year 3 Total	Year 4 Hours/week	Year 4 Weeks/year	Year 4 Total	Year 5 Hours/week	Year 5 Weeks/year	Year 5 Total
Marketing															
Sales/deliveries	10	30	300	10	30	300	20	30	600	20	30	600	30	30	900
Promotion	10	5	50	10	5	50	10	5	50	10	5	50	10	5	50
Marketing Total	**20**	**35**	**350**	**20**	**35**	**350**	**30**	**35**	**650**	**30**	**35**	**650**	**40**	**35**	**950**
Operations															
Farm Manager	40	52	2080	40	52	2080	40	52	2080	40	52	2080	40	52	2080
Farm volunteers (Crop management)	60	52	3120	60	52	3120	60	52	3120	60	52	3120	60	52	3120
Farm volunteers (harvest)	60	30	1800	90	30	2700	90	30	2700	120	30	3600	120	30	3600
Construction volunteers (Hoop houses)	240	2	480	240	2	480	240	2	480	240	2	480			
Operations Total	**400**	**136**	**7480**	**430**	**136**	**8380**	**430**	**136**	**8380**	**460**	**136**	**9280**	**220**	**134**	**8800**

Example Worksheet # 20 – Manpower Needs

Task	Year 1			Year 2			Year 3			Year 4			Year 5		
	Hours/ week	Weeks/ year	Total	Hours/ week	Weeks/ year	Total	Hours/ week	Weeks/ year	Total	Hours/ week	Weeks/ year	Total	Hours/ week	Weeks/ year	Total
Administrative															
Administrative services (Town X CDC)	4	50	200	4	50	200	4	50	200	4	50	200	4	50	200
Administrative Total	**4**	**50**	**200**	**4**	**50**	**200**	**4**	**50**	**200**	**4**	**50**	**200**	**4**	**50**	**200**
Financial															
Financial services (Town X CDC)	4	50	200	4	50	200	4	50	200	4	50	200	4	50	
Financial Total	**4**	**50**	**200**	**4**	**50**	**200**	**4**	**50**	**200**	**4**	**50**	**200**	**4**	**50**	**200**

Note: *Manpower will need to be re-evaluated by the Farm Manager and Director of Town X CDC as the farm is brought into production. Initial manpower needs may be higher in order to set-up the facility and begin operations.*

Example Worksheet # 21 – Workforce Needs

Describe the manpower needed to operate the farm. This should include management, as well as farm labor.

Position description	What skills or experience are needed?	How will positions be filled (e.g., full-time, part-time, volunteer, service contractor)?	What benefits will be offered?	Typical salary range
Farm manager.	Knowledge of farm management, three season growing using hoop houses and vertical gardens, and organic farming techniques.	Full-time.	?	$35,000 to $40,000 per year.
Farm workers.	No specific skills or experience required.	Part-time volunteers.	None.	None.
Promotion.	Knowledge of advertising and graphics.	Part-time volunteers.	None.	None.
Sales and distribution.	Experience in sales, drivers license and vehicle.	Part-time volunteers.	None.	None.
General workers.	Basic skills in construction for assembly of hoop houses.	Part-time volunteers.	None.	None.
Administrative support.	Basic administrative skills.	Part-time – will be filled by existing Toledo CDC employees.	Existing benefits.	Existing salary.
Financial support.	Basic financial skills.	Part-time – will be filled by existing Toledo CDC employees.	Existing benefits.	Existing salary.

What training will be required and how will it be accomplished?

Training will be accomplished by the farm manager for all farm workers. Sales, promotion, and delivery training will be provided by Town X CDC.

Example Worksheet # 22 – Regulation and Policy

Identify the type of permits, licenses, regulations, or certifications and associated fees required to start up and conduct the business.

What regulatory requirements exist? What conditions or issues are associated with each requirement? What fees will be incurred? Can the requirement be met?

Regulatory Issue	Requirement	Conditions or Issues	Fees ($)	Can it be met?
Planning.	Planning approval is required and has been received.	No conditions.	No Fees.	Yes.
Zoning.	Property zoning includes agricultural uses.	No conditions.	No Fees.	Yes.
Waste handling and disposal.	No specific waste handling requirements; however, composting may require approvals.			
Health.				
Safety.	Federal and state worker safety will need to be considered for employees and labor.			Yes.
Building.	Building permits will be needed for all structures.			Yes.
Inspections.	Inspections will be required for new construction.			Yes.
Environmental.	Environmental issues have been addressed through the State Voluntary Action Program. Site assessment and remedial action are complete.	Native soil cannot be used for crop production, concrete pads must remain.	No.	Yes.

Example Worksheet # 22 – Regulation and Policy

What regulatory requirements exist? What conditions or issues are associated with each requirement? What fees will be incurred? Can the requirement be met?

Regulatory Issue	Requirement	Conditions or Issues	Fees ($)	Can it be met?
Food handling (handling, storing, packaging, and distributing).				
Business operations.				
Sales tax.				
Other (itemize).				

Note: *Additional information will need to be obtained in order to identify regulatory issues.*

Example Worksheet # 23 – Annual Expenses

Estimate the annual expenses for the farm.

Detailed Expenses	Year 1	Year 2	Year 3	Year 4	Year 5	Assumptions
						Assumption for annual adjustment for inflation percentage.
						Identify any additional assumptions used to develop the expense estimates.
Direct Farm Operating Costs						
Annual setup and removal						
Hoop house-temporary	-	-	-	-	-	Hoop houses to be permanent - One-time cost for installation.
Vertical garden	100	100	100	100	100	Vertical gardens will be installed by volunteers or farm manager, cost for miscellaneous items for set-up.
Other						
Total annual setup and removal	100	100	100	100	100	
Repairs and Maintenance						
Repairs and Maintenance	1,000	1,000	1,000	2,000	2,000	Minor repairs to hoop houses and raised beds.
Total repairs and maintenance	1,000	1,000	1,000	2,000	2,000	
Equipment and Tools						
Fuel	-	-	-	-	-	No fuel use is anticipated.
Equipment leases (long-term)	-	-	-	-	-	No leases anticipated.
Rentals (short-term or daily)	-	-	-	-	-	No rentals anticipated.
Processing equipment	-	-	-	-	-	No processing equipment anticipated.
Tools	100	100	100	100	100	Annual expenditure to replaced worn or broken tools.
Tractor	-	-	-	-	-	No tractor anticipated.

Example Worksheet # 23 – Annual Expenses

Detailed Expenses		Year 1	Year 2	Year 3	Year 4	Year 5	Assumptions
Truck		-	-	-	-	-	A truck or delivery vehicle may be needed but not anticipated in first five years.
Other							
	Total equipment	100	100	100	100	100	
Seed & Soil Materials							
Fertilizers and pesticides		100	200	300	400	400	Soil condition and pest control is anticipated through soil management techniques.
Seed/seedlings		100	200	300	400	400	Seeds and seedlings will be donated or seedlings started at farm.
Soil preparation		-	1,000	1,000	500	500	Assume compost will be generated on site in later years.
Supplies		900	1,000	1,500	1,800	2,000	
Other							
	Total materials	1,100	2,400	3,100	3,100	3,300	
Human Resources & Personnel							
Direct Farm Payroll							
Manager salaries		31,200	31,200	31,200	31,200	31,200	Assumed $15.00 per hour for 2080 hours per year.
Hourly payroll		-	-	-	-	-	Additional labor is assumed to be volunteer.
Temporary workers		-	-	-	-	-	Additional labor is assumed to be volunteer.
Benefits		1,560	1,560	1,560	1,560	1,560	Assumed to be 5% of salary.
Workers compensation insurance		1,872	1,872	1,872	1,872	1,872	Assumed to be 6% of salary.
Payroll taxes		6,240	6,240	6,240	6,240	6,240	Assumed to be 20% of salary.
Payroll service fees		-	-	-	-	-	Assumed to be covered by Town X CDC.
Volunteer expenses		2,000	2,000	3,000	3,000	3,000	Miscellaneous costs for volunteers.
Administrative payroll		-	-	-	-	-	Assumed to be covered by Town X CDC.

Example Worksheet # 23 – Annual Expenses

Detailed Expenses	Year 1	Year 2	Year 3	Year 4	Year 5	Assumptions
Training and professional development	500	500	500	500	500	Cost to attend conferences/training session for Farm Manager.
Professional						
Accounting	–	–	–	–	–	Assumed to be covered by Town X CDC.
Consulting	–	–	–	–	–	Assumed to be covered by Town X CDC.
Contractors	–	–	–	–	–	Assumed to be covered by Town X CDC.
Legal	–	–	–	–	–	Assumed to be covered by Town X CDC.
Other						
Total human resources	**43,372**	**43,372**	**44,372**	**44,372**	**44,372**	
Sales and Distribution						
Delivery	–	–	–	–	–	Assumed to be handled by volunteers.
Fuel, travel & vehicles	300	300	300	400	400	Volunteer fuel reimbursement.
Packaging materials (crates, bags)	1,000	1,000	1,500	2,000	2,000	Bags and/or crates for produce.
Storage	–	–	–	–	–	No storage anticipated.
Rent	–	–	–	–	–	No rent anticipated.
Other						
Total sales and distribution	**1,300**	**1,300**	**1,800**	**2,400**	**2,400**	
Marketing and Advertising						
Advertising	300	300	300	300	300	Marketing materials.
Direct marketing	300	300	300	300	300	Marketing materials.
Mailing and advertising supplies	300	300	300	300	300	Marketing communications.
Postage	500	500	500	500	500	Periodic mailers to 1000 plus.
Public and press relations						
Signs	150	150	150	150	150	New and replacement signs - materials only - labor assumed to be volunteer.

Example Worksheet # 23 – Annual Expenses

Detailed Expenses	Year 1	Year 2	Year 3	Year 4	Year 5	Assumptions
Web site and web advertising	500	500	500	500	500	Assumed to be maintained by Town X CDC and volunteers.
Licensing						
Other		500	500	500	500	Volunteer expense reimbursement.
Total marketing and advertising	2,050	2,050	2,050	2,050	2,050	
Utilities						
Electric	2,000	2,000	2,000	2,000	2,000	
Telephone	1,200	1,200	1,200	1,200	1,200	Cell phone for farm manager.
Water	500	600	750	800	800	
Sewer	600	600	600	600	600	
Heat (oil, gas)	1,000	1,800	1,800	1,800	1,800	
Total utilities	5,300	6,200	6,350	6,400	6,400	
General and Administrative						
Bank Charges	-	-	-	-	-	
Computers	-	-	-	-	-	
Insurance						
Liability	2,000	2,000	2,000	2,000	2,000	
Property & Casualty	2,000	2,000	2,000	2,000	2,000	
Licenses, permits, and fees						
Miscellaneous	-	-	-	-	-	
Office equipment	-	-	-	-	-	
Postage	500	500	500	500	500	
Rent and leases	-	-	-	-	-	
Supplies	500	500	500	500	500	
Taxes - entity or corporation						
Taxes - property						

Example Worksheet # 23 – Annual Expenses

Detailed Expenses	Year 1	Year 2	Year 3	Year 4	Year 5	Assumptions
Other						
Total general and administrative	5,000	5,000	5,000	5,000	5,000	
One-Time or Start-up Costs						
Deposits with public utilities						
Promotion for opening	1,550					Community recruitment, opening ceremony (Based on Market Study estimate).
Signs	150					Initial signs and log development (Based on Market Study estimate).
Web ordering system						
Other Site Cleanup, shrub and tree removal	1,000					
Initial Soil/Compost for beds	5,000	5,000	5,000	5,000	-	Initial cost for soil/compost to set up beds in new hoop houses.
Total start-up costs	7,700	5,000	5,000	5,000	-	
Non-cash expenses						
Depreciation	-	-	-	-	-	
Total non-cash expenses	-	-	-	-	-	

Example Worksheet # 24 – Projected Income

Detailed Income	Year 1	Year 2	Year 3	Year 4	Year 5	Assumptions and Limitations
Farm Sales						
Retail	10,315	19,275	28,877	32,658	27,170	Assumed 100%, 100%, 85%, 75%, 65% of sales in year 1, 2, 3, 4, 5, respectively.
Wholesale	-	-	5,096	11,219	15,707	Assumed 0%, 0%, 15%, 25%, 35% of sales in year 1, 2, 3, 4, 5, respectively.
Other programs	-	-	-	2,000	2,000	CSA Income from retail sales.
Less: Spoilage	103	193	340	459	449	Assumed to be 1% of crop.
Net Projected Sales	10,419	19,468	34,313	46,336	45,326	
Other sources of Income						
Grants						
USDA Grant	35,000	30,000	25,000	20,000	15,000	Initial year based on Market Research proposal. Assumed reduce funding in subsequent years.
Local Grants	10,000	5,000	5,000	5,000	5,000	Initial year based on Market Research proposal. Assumed reduce funding in subsequent years.
Donations						
Special Events (Source)	3,000	3,000	3,000	3,000	3,000	Initial year based on Market Research proposal.
Interest income	-	-	-	-	-	
Rental income	-	-	-	-	-	
Total other income	48,000	38,000	33,000	28,000	23,000	

Example Worksheet # 25 – Income and Expense

Estimate the annual profit or loss for the farm.

Profit & Loss Projection	Year 1	Year 2	Year 3	Year 4	Year 5
Income					
Projected Sales	10,419	19,468	34,313	46,336	45,326
Grants and other income	48,000	38,000	33,000	28,000	23,000
Total Income	58,419	57,468	67,313	74,336	68,326
Direct Operating Expenses					
Annual setup and removal	100	100	100	100	100
Total repairs and maintenance	1,000	1,000	1,000	2,000	2,000
Equipment and Tools	100	100	100	100	100
Seed & Soil Materials	1,100	2,400	3,100	3,100	3,300
Human Resources & Personnel	43,372	43,372	44,372	44,372	44,372
subtotal	45,672	46,972	48,672	49,672	49,872
Indirect Operating Expenses					
Sales and Distribution	1,300	1,300	1,800	2,400	2,400
Marketing and Advertising	2,050	2,050	2,050	2,050	2,050
Utilities	5,300	6,200	6,350	6,400	6,400
Total Operating Expenses	54,322	46,850	49,200	50,850	51,050
Net Operating Income(Loss)	**4,097**	**946**	**8,441**	**13,814**	**7,604**
General and Administrative	5,000	5,000	5,000	5,000	5,000
One-Time or Start-up Costs	7,700	5,000	5,000	5,000	-
Net Income Before Non-Cash Items	(8,603)	(9,054)	(1,559)	3,814	2,604
Depreciation and other non-cash expenses	-	-	-	-	-
Net Income Before Taxes	(8,603)	618	8,113	13,486	12,276
Income Taxes (if any)					

Example Worksheet # 25 – Income and Expense

Profit & Loss Projection	Year 1	Year 2	Year 3	Year 4	Year 5
Net Income (Loss)		(9,672)	(9,672)	(9,672)	(9,672)

Example Worksheet # 26 – Projected Fixed Assets

Estimate the fixed assets for the farm.

Fixed Assets	Year 1	Year 2	Year 3	Year 4	Year 5	Assumptions
						Identify any assumptions used to develop the expense estimates.
						(Building and site prep estimates based on January 2011 preliminary project cost estimate.)
Initial Cash Outlay for Fixed Asset						
Land (Purchase or Lease)	-	-	-	-	-	
Site preparation	188,000					
Hoop house (including construction labor)[3]	16,000	16,000	16,000	16,000	-	Labor assumed to be performed by volunteers.
Raised beds/planters	2,250	2,250	2,250	2,250	-	Labor assumed to be performed by volunteers.
Vertical garden hardware	4,500	-	-	-	-	Labor assumed to be performed by volunteers.
Buildings and other structures (Itemize)	297,000					Educational Facility.
Sales shed or farmstand			40,000	162,000		Enclosed farm stand, Shed.
Equipment (Itemize)						Installation of electric and water for hoop houses, repair of fences and installation of gates.
Other	5,000	1,000	1,000	1,000	-	
Total outlays for fixed assets	512,750	19,250	59,250	181,250	-	

---

[3] It is assumed that four Hoop Houses will be built on the site over four years as outlined under Example Worksheet #5 – Goals.

Example Worksheet # 27 – Projected Funding

Estimate the funding sources for the farm.

Available Capital	Year 1	Year 2	Year 3	Year 4	Year 5	Assumptions and Limitations
						Identify any assumptions used to develop the expense estimates or limitations on the use of grants, donations or other funds.
Grants						
County Port Authority	28,500		10,000	10,000		Development and Administration grant.
State Community Development Finance Fund	20,000		10,000	20,000		Received – Site preparation, building construction, storage building.
Local Foundation Grant	35,000					Potential – Purchase of hoop houses.
CDBG	437,000			106,000		Potential – Site development, education center, farm stand.
USDA Grant: Community Food Project		10,000	15,000	20,000		Potential – Provide funding for capital improvements, hoop houses.
Donations						
Nonprofit Food Technology	7,000		15,000	15,000		Donation of vertical garden equipment, hoop houses.
Local donations and Fund raising events	10,000	10,000	10,000	10,000	10,000	Offset portion of farm manger salary.
Loans						
Investment						
Financing						
Other sources of capital						
Total available capital	537,500	20,000	60,000	181,000	10,000	

Example Worksheet # 28 – Funding Information

Describe the sources of funding (capital) to purchase and install the fixed assets needed to start up the farm and achieve the business plan.

What are the potential sources of funding?
Funding for Site preparation, hoop houses, education facility and storage building - Department of Housing and Urban Development (HUD) Community Development Block Grant (CDBG).   County Port Authority.   *Nonprofit Food Technology*.   Local donations and fund raising events.
Are there specific limitations on the funding?
HUD CDGB funds can be used for the improvement of communities through assistance to low- to moderate-income persons and addressing slum and blight.
What are the critical assumptions concerning the funding?
Funding is available and can be obtained within the time constraints for construction.   HUD CDGB funds will be invested in public facility activities that will spur further economic investment and maximize job creation/retention.
What is the timing of the funding and how will it impact the achievement of the business plan?
It is essential that funding be obtained in late fall in order to ensure that improvements are in place for the growing season.
How will the funding be obtained?
HUD CDGB funding will be obtained through a grant application to Town X.   Funding applications will be submitted to appropriate funding source.   Fund raising events will be held on the farm at area community facilities.
Are there expenses associated with the funding?
There will be administrative expenses in developing the information needed for the applications and preparing the applications for the grant funding.   There will be costs for fund raising events.

Example Worksheet # 29 – Risk Management

Identify and evaluate potential risks that can impact the financial strategy and the success of the business plan.

What are the potential risks that may need to be managed?	How likely is the risk to occur (high, medium, low)?	What is planned to minimize potential risks if they occur?
Production: Crop failure or unusually small yields.	High - Smaller than planned yield rates are likely during the first few years.	Farm Manager's primary objective during the first few years will be to implement cultivation techniques that minimize overhead and maximize production. This will be accomplished with support from the University of Town X, *Nonprofit Food Technology*, and Town X Grows.
Marketing: Unable to sell full production.	Medium.	Focused promotion and marketing approach. Utilize volunteers to interact with potential customers.
Financial: Unable to obtain sufficient funding to sustain the first three to four years and to fund growth.	High.	Incorporate fund raising using events at the farm and focus effort to obtain federal, state, and/or private funding.
Labor: Unable to find sufficient volunteers and maintain consistent labor force. Performance of Farm Manager.	Medium.	Utilize educational activities at local high schools and trade schools, and the University of Town X, and solicit neighborhood and community groups for support and volunteer time.
Other.